GRAINS

by Robin Nelson

Lerner Publications Company · Minneapolis

We need to eat many kinds of food to be **healthy**.

We need to eat foods in
the **grains** group.

Grains are bread, cereal,
rice, and pasta.

Grains give us **vitamins** and **minerals**.

Grains help food move
through our body.

Grains give us energy.

We need six **servings** of
grains each day.

We can eat bread.

We can eat waffles.

We can eat tortillas.

We can eat cornflakes.

We can eat oatmeal.

We can eat rice.

We can eat spaghetti.

We can eat pretzels.

Grains keep me healthy.

Fats, Oils, and Sweets
Use Sparingly

**Milk, Yogurt, and
Cheese Group**
2-3 Servings

**Meat, Poultry, Fish,
Dry Beans, Eggs,
and Nuts Group**
2-3 Servings

**Vegetable
Group**
3-5 Servings

Fruit Group
2-4 Servings

Bread, Cereal, Rice, and Pasta Group
6-11 Servings

Bread, Cereal, Rice, and Pasta Group

The food pyramid shows us how many servings of different foods we should eat every day. The bread, cereal, rice, and pasta group is on the bottom level of the food pyramid. The foods in this group are called grains. This part of the pyramid is the biggest because you need the most food from this group. You need to eat 6-11 servings of grains every day. Grains give you energy and make you strong.

Grains Facts

 Grains come from plants—mostly wheat, corn, rice, and oats.

 Cereal, bread, and pasta are made from wheat. A new kind of concrete is also made from wheat.

 White bread is good for you, but whole wheat bread is better for you. It has more fiber, which is very good for you.

There are many different kinds of pasta. You could try spaghetti, macaroni, angel hair, ziti, ravioli, fettuccine, or even bow tie.

 The average person in China consumes a pound of rice a day.

 More foods are made from wheat than any other grain.

Glossary

 grains – seeds of wheat, corn, rice, or oats

 healthy – not sick; well

 minerals – parts of food that keep your blood, bones, and teeth healthy

 servings – amounts of food

 vitamins – parts of food that keep your body healthy

Index

The photographs in this book are reproduced through the courtesy of: © Todd Strand/IPS, front cover, pp. 4, 12, 13, 14, 17; © PhotoDisc/Royalty-Free, pp. 2, 5, 7, 9, 10, 22 (second from top, middle, bottom); © Wheat Foods Council, pp. 3, 8, 11, 15, 16, 22 (top, second from bottom); © Corbis Royalty-Free Images, p. 6.

Illustration on page 18 by Bill Hauser.

Lerner Publications Company
A division of Lerner Publishing Group
241 First Avenue North
Minneapolis, MN 55401 USA

Website address: www.lernerbooks.com

Library of Congress Cataloging-in-Publication Data

Nelson, Robin, 1971–
    Grains / by Robin Nelson.
      p.   cm. — (First step nonfiction)
    Summary: An introduction to different grain products and the part they play in a healthy diet.
    ISBN: 0–8225–4628–0 (lib. bdg. : alk. paper)
    1. Cereals as food—Juvenile literature. 2. Grain—Juvenile literature. [1. Grain.
    2. Nutrition.] I. Title. II. Series.
    TX393 .N45 2003
    641.3'31—dc21   2002013617

Manufactured in the United States of America
1 2 3 4 5 6 – JR – 08 07 06 05 04 03